Ch

Chosen!

A confirmation book for teenage girls

Susan **Hardwick**

First published in 2000 by
KEVIN MAYHEW LTD
Buxhall
Stowmarket
Suffolk IP14 3BW

0 1 2 3 4 5 6 7 8 9

ISBN 1 84003 497 1
Catalogue No 1500329

Cover design by Jonathan Stroulger
Typesetting by Elisabeth Bates
Printed and bound in Great Britain

Contents

The First Word _____

'Hi! – I'm Emma.'

'Hiya! My name's Roxie – well, Roxanne, really. But I'll usually only answer to Roxie. Emma is my best mate, and you might remember us from "Upside Down"*.'

'And we hope you like this book, as well. It's especially for teenagers like us who have been confirmed – and, maybe, baptised as well. The first part is about our confirmation . . .'

'And my baptism.'

'OK, OK. I hadn't forgotten! – Roxie was baptised and confirmed at the same service.'

'The second part talks about what baptism, confirmation, communion, and various other things, is/are/is . . . which is it?'

'Is, I guess.'

'Anyway, in Part Three, there are prayers on all sorts of subjects. And there's a whole section on ways to pray – ever so interesting, actually, and not at all boring.'

'And the final part is called "Looking Forward", and is about being a follower of Jesus. As I said already – hope you like it. Happy reading!'

'Yes. Ditto. Ta-ta! See you around.'

'Bye!'

Emma   Roxie

*Upside Down – Prayers for teenage girls, by Susan Hardwick, published by Kevin Mayhew Publishers, 1998.

PART ONE

Anticipation _____

'There! What do you think?' Roxanne stood back and surveyed her handiwork.

Emma looked critically at her reflection in the mirror. 'Mmmm. Not sure,' she said, doubtfully.

'*I* think it looks ace. Really great. Well? Do you want me to do it like that for you tomorrow, or not?'

Emma turned her head this way and that, still watching her reflection as she did so. 'I *think* so', she said at last. 'Yes. It's wicked!'

She nodded her head vigorously as she spoke. It proved the wrong thing to do. The precariously swirled and swathed hair gave way to gravity and fell about her shoulders, scattering clips all over the floor.

'Honestly! You shouldn't have moved like that', exclaimed Roxanne in exasperation, flopping down on her bed. 'That took me *ages*'.

She put her hands behind her head, her feet up on the wall, and gazed dreamily at the ceiling.

'Oh, Roxie, what a shame. I'm sorry. Really I am', said Emma, trying to stifle a gurgle of laughter. She flung herself down on the other bed, and joined Roxanne in contemplating the ceiling.

'Looking forward to tomorrow?' Roxie asked.

'Mmmm! Oh, yes. You?'

'You bet. Can't wait. I wonder if we'll feel – you know, *different*'. Roxanne turned on her side towards Emma, and propped her head on her hand. 'I read this article recently', she continued, 'about someone who was confirmed. He told about how, when the Bishop laid hands upon his head, he felt all sorts of things.

He said that a real hot heat started in his head, then flowed right through the whole of his body, making him feel peaceful all over. And sort of "pulled together", as if all the different bits of him had been united into one. And a great sense of being loved by God, and . . . and . . . I can't remember the rest. But he said it was *a-mazing*. I really wish that'd happen to me.' She sighed wistfully. 'Probably won't, though. It'll probably happen to *you*, because you've been at it a heap longer than I have.'

'I beg your pardon?' said Emma, pulling a mock prim expression.

'You know what I mean', laughed Roxie. 'Being a Christian, and all that. You've been one for ever.'

'Well – perhaps if we want it enough, it'll happen like that for *both* of us', said Emma. 'It's always saying in the Bible about asking and, if it's God's will, it'll be so. God would surely want us to feel something special at our confirmation.'

'Right. Here goes.' Roxanne closed her eyes and concentrated. 'Dear God, I really, really, *really* want so much for Emma and me to feel something extra-special at the moment of our confirmation tomorrow. If it is your will, please may it be so. Thanking you in advance. I love you. Your grateful friend, Roxie. Amen.'

'Amen', said Emma, joining herself to the prayer. 'Do . . . ?'

'And, God, whilst we're on the "thank you's", continued Roxanne, ignoring Emma and warming to her subject, 'thank you for calling me to serve you. Thank you for using Emma to tell me about you. Thank you for coming into my life and changing it, and me. Thank you that I have Emma as my best friend. Amen. It's OK, I've finished now', she added. 'Go on, then. What're you going to say?'

But before Emma could reply, there was a tap on the door of Roxie's room. Roxie jumped up and opened it. Her boyfriend stood there, lounging against the door frame.

'Hi, you!' she said, with a pleased smile.

'Hi, you', he smiled back. 'Hi, Emma.'

'Hi, Darren.'

'You both ready for tomorrow, then?' he asked.

'Yup. You?'

'Yeah. I feel kind of weird and fidgety, though – like I can't settle. I bought you these.' He presented Roxie with twelve roses. 'For your confirmation.'

'Oh, Darren! They're beautiful. Thank you!' she exclaimed, giving him a hug. 'I got something for you, but I'll give it to you tomorrow. OK? What're you wearing tomorrow?' she asked in a muffled voice, as she buried her face in the flowers in order to smell the perfume better.

'Mum's going on about me wearing a suit, but I was thinking of my new black jeans and black shirt. What do you think?'

'Yeah. Oh, yeah – your jeans and shirt. They look mint. No. Wear your suit. Yes, wear your suit – with your black shirt.'

'Yes, ma'am', he drawled, grinning as he gave her a mock salute. He turned to Emma. 'Tony coming tomorrow, then?'

'No. Don't think so', sighed Emma. 'I asked him, but he said he'd feel a hypocrite going to something he didn't believe in. I'd *really* like him to be there, though.' Her boyfriend's lack of interest in the thing that was so important to her was a cause of much sadness and longing for Emma. Her faith was central to her existence, and to her understanding of who she was and how she should live her life. It was the thing, more than any other, which guided and sustained her. She so wished Tony could understand; that it could be something they could share. 'He said he'd be thinking of me, though,' she added defensively.

'Big deal', retorted Roxie, loyally. 'You should tell him he's just *got* to be there. I would, if it was me – wouldn't I, Darren?'

Darren grinned again. 'I'm off,' he said. 'I'm meeting the lads for a quick game of footie. See you tomorrow.' He clattered off down the stairs, and Roxie sat down next to her friend. She could see from Emma's downcast expression how disappointed she was about Tony, and she put her arm around Emma's shoulder.

'I want him to come because he wants to be there. Not because of some dreary obligation to me,' Emma sighed.

'Cheer up', Roxie comforted. 'I guess he doesn't realise how much it all means to you. *I* wouldn't have done, 'till it happened to *me*. Until it happens to you, you can't understand what people're going on about when they talk about a "God of Love" – and "asking Jesus into your life" – and "a new way of living and being". And "praying" – Hey, remember? That's how it all really began for me. Remember? Do you?' Roxie repeated, shaking Emma's shoulder as she tried to distract Emma's thoughts. '*I'd* been feeling all kind of empty and not exactly miserable but not happy either, for ages. But *you* seemed to have something really special. A kind of strength in you, to help you through all the muddly and confusing times – not that you didn't get times like that too. But *you* seemed to know where you were going, as if you had a sort of inner map you were following. Then, one day, when I was feeling *really* fed up, and had got into trouble *again* at school, *and* at home, I thought to myself, "this is *rubbish*. I'm being really sad. I want what Emma's got." So I asked you if there was a secret to praying. And did people have to go on a course to Learn How to Pray, or something.'

'Yeah. I remember', nodded Emma, smiling. 'I said that anyone could pray, and that it was the easiest thing in the world.'

'And *I* asked you if you'd show me.'

'And *I* said, "OK. If you want." Then I went on about prayer being something you can do any time. That it's like conversations between you and me. We're best friends and we tell each other everything; all our biggest secrets we wouldn't tell anyone else – and that prayer is like that.'

'You said that it's like God's your very best friend, who you can tell everything to – all the best and all the worst things – just the way it really is, just the way it really feels', Roxie put in.

'Also', added Emma, 'that prayer reminds me that God loves me, however I feel. However much I change, God's love is always constant, so . . .'

'And *I* said', Roxanne interrupted once again, '"You mean I should talk to God like I talk to you? Even when I'm mad at you?"'

'And *I* said', laughed Emma, 'that talking to God was like one of our phone conversations. Sometimes I talk and you listen. Sometimes it's the other way round. If one of us talked all the time, and the other couldn't get a word in edgeways, it wouldn't be much of a conversation, would it? So it's important to listen as well . . .'

'. . . And not to jabber on and on and on, like I sometimes do – I know.'

'Then you asked me if God ever answered me back, and told me stuff that I didn't know before', said Emma.

'And you said', Roxie added, '"You bet! You wouldn't believe some of the things . . . !" It's true, though', she continued, earnestly, 'I've found it out for myself. And the most exciting thing is that when you pray you really do find that things change. Not always in the way you think or expect they will, but usually in the way that turns out to be for the best.' Roxie gave her friend a hug. 'Thanks, Emma! If it hadn't been for you . . .'

'I guess God would have got through to you, one way or another', Emma replied, returning the hug. 'I'm just so glad he used me. Hey! You're not really going to wear those shoes tomorrow, are you?' she asked as she spied over Roxie's shoulder a pair of high-fashion, but extremely precarious, shoes under the dressing table.

'Why not? They're beautiful!'

'Mmmm. They're ace. But you'll probably topple off them at a vital moment, and fall into the font, or land in the Bishop's lap, or something.' Both girls giggled at the thought. Emma chewed her lip. 'Talking of what we're wearing, I'm worried I've put on weight on my bum, and that those trousers we bought specially are going to be too tight. If I put the whole lot on, you can tell me what you think. I've brought a skirt with me, as well. Just in case.' Emma changed into the proposed outfit, and Roxanne surveyed her with a critical eye.

'Turn round. Nope. They're fine. And they look *really* nice with that top and those boots.' She pulled out her shoes from under the dressing table. 'I'd better practise a bit more with these. I don't want to be giving the Bishop a heart attack.'

Sometime later, before they went to bed, at Roxie's suggestion they read once more through the baptism and confirmation service, and what they were going to have to say.

'I wish I'd been baptised as a baby,' sighed Roxanne. 'Then there wouldn't be both to do now.'

'Yeah, but remember what Liz said when she was preparing us – that originally baptism and confirmation were done together,' Emma reminded her. 'Hey. Where're your notes?' After a brief hunt, Roxie extricated them from a pile of underwear. They found the appropriate place, and Emma read out what was written.

'". . . it was only when Christian communities got scattered so widely, and the few bishops there were then could only get round them all once every few years, that the custom began for people to be baptised when they were ready. Then, when the Bishop came round eventually, he would do all the backlog of confirmations. However, sometimes, there were years and years in between people being baptised and confirmed." There you are, Roxie. By having them both done together, you're actually doing it the way it was originally meant to be.'

'Oh, yes', said Roxie, brightening, 'I'd forgotten all that. Aahh. Poor you, Emma. You've done it all wrong!' Emma picked up a pillow and thumped Roxie with it. Roxie responded, and soon they were having a very satisfactory and enjoyable pillowfight.

Emma lay in her bed, gazing into the soft darkness. Roxie was sound asleep and Emma could hear her even breathing.

She thought of her life up until this moment. It had been just like a journey, containing both good and bad times, good and bad things – a winding road that had run through some nice, some not-so-nice and, on occasions, some really gross places.

Sometimes the going had been so hard and difficult, like wading through mud on a very cloudy day. And, sometimes, it had been like walking on soft springy grass or sand, with the sun shining warmly and birds singing their hearts out with their joy in the beauty of creation. There had been hills and hilltops, and there had been valleys.

The biggest valley had been when her brother had been killed. Then her faith sometimes seemed to have been the only thing which had kept her going.

But, whether she was happy or sad, she knew that Jesus had always been – and would continue always to be – her most faithful and constant and loving companion. He was closer to her than she was to herself. He would never, ever let her down; never, ever leave her. And being confirmed was her way of saying thank you. It was her way of saying that she wanted to give her life over to him completely – just as he had given his life for love of her, when he had died upon the cross.

Emma's eyes closed, and she slipped into sleep.

Today's the day! ───────────────

A beam of sunlight slanted through a chink in the curtains and shone onto the beds of the two sleeping girls. Roxie woke first. She yawned, rubbed her eyes, slowly and luxuriously stretched first one limb and then the other, like a cat, and then looked over at Emma. She was still fast asleep, lying on her back with an arm outstretched in her usual abandoned fashion.

Roxie was glad Emma had slept over last night. It was so much more fun and special sharing all of this together. Before she'd met Emma, Roxie had thought that Christians were a bit sad, and that they went to church because they hadn't anything more interesting or exciting to do with their time. But then Emma had come into her life. Laughing Emma, bubbling over with fun and in love with life – *and* a Christian. She didn't seem to care when other kids teased her, or were mocking about her beliefs. Sometimes she would answer, and sometimes she would just ignore it and them, depending upon what had been said and whether she thought it was worth a reply.

At first, Roxie had been one of those who teased her. But, bit by bit, she had been drawn to this girl who had the courage to declare what she believed and who would not back down in the face of ridicule. And Emma didn't just wear Christianity as a kind of badge or label – she lived it. She would always be one of the first to scrape up anyone who had fallen down in the playground. And she would stand shoulder to shoulder with anyone being bullied, and try to defend them.

It was on just such an occasion that her and Emma's friendship had really begun. Ros, one of the most awkward and least popular pupils, had been clowning around in a really silly way, in order to make one or two people nearby laugh. Their amusement encouraged her to be increasingly silly and extreme, until a crowd had gathered around, cheering and clapping – and sneering.

Roxie remembered how she'd stood silently in the the middle of the crowd, more and more uneasy about it all, but not sure what to do about it. The next moment, Emma was standing beside Ros, facing the jeering crowd with her eyes blazing. Roxie had never seen Emma so angry before.

'Leave her alone!' she'd cried. 'Go away, and leave her alone!' But some had persisted, and the rest had stayed, fascinated to see the outcome. Roxie had felt herself propelled forward, as if an invisible hand was pushing against her back, until she was standing on the other side of Ros.

'Yes! Back off, you sad lot!' she had shouted. *'You're* the ones who are pathetic!'

Faced by the two angry girls, who had been united by the common purpose of sticking up for the now-drooping Ros, the crowd began to drift shamefacedly away, until only the three girls were left. Roxie remembered how Emma had then said to Ros how, if she didn't respect herself, no one else would, and told her that making a fool of herself in order to gain attention definitely was not the best way of getting noticed. Emma had also suggested that perhaps the two of them could spend a bit of time together talking about it all – if that was what Ros wanted. Ros had not acted stupid again. And her chats with Emma had borne fruit to the extent that her respect for herself and, there-fore her confidence, had grown. Before long, she was a whole heap calmer, and also had made some more friends.

From the day of the playground incident, Roxie and Emma had been inseparable. Roxie had learnt that the teasing and ridicule about her faith had hurt Emma a lot after all, although she had never publicly shown it. Sometimes, it had even reduced her to shed some strictly private tears. Roxie's curiosity had been aroused. What was it about all this Christianity stuff, that meant Emma was prepared to put up with the mindless teasing? But it wasn't just that. Emma was different – not in a stupid way, though. It was difficult to put your finger on it exactly. She was, sort of, more 'together' than many girls of their age. In all this weird, confusing, upside-down and inside-out time of being a teenager, Emma seemed to have something special to hang on to, to help her decide about things and to make sense of them. She was . . . she was herself. With Emma, you got the real Emma.

Roxie liked the way Emma didn't push her beliefs down your throat, though she was very happy to talk about her faith if you asked her to. Once, Emma had shyly confided in Roxie that she really tried to talk about her faith through the way she lived and how she was with people, rather than just using words, because words on their own couldn't convey all that she felt in her heart . . .

All these memories tumbled through Roxie's mind as she yawned and lazily stretched again. It was a good day when Emma came into my life, she reflected. She's the best mate ever. Getting out of bed, Roxie tiptoed over to the washbasin, held her flannel under the cold water tap, then tiptoed over to where Emma lay sleeping.

Emma dreamed she was lying out under a gorgeous hot sun when, suddenly, out of the clear blue sky, icy flakes of snow began to fall on her. She awoke with a start, freezing cold drops of water splashing down onto her face, to Roxie's delighted grin at Emma's shriek. 'Wakey, wakey!' Roxie said. 'Today's the day!' Emma lay still for a moment, then suddenly sat up, grabbed the flannel and stuffed it down the front of the giant T-shirt Roxie wore to sleep in. 'Serve you right!' she laughed, in reponse to Roxie's anguished squeal. Grabbing her wash-things, she exited quickly to the bathroom, leaving Roxie trying frantically to extricate the freezing flannel, whilst keeping it as far as possible away from her warm skin.

Emma, Roxie and Darren sat with the other confirmation candidates at the front of the church. Several churches had come together to share the confirmation, and so the candidates filled several pews. Roxie had been relieved to find out at the rehearsal, which had taken place a few days previously, that she was not the only one to be baptised before being confirmed. Scattered around the full church were the proudly beaming parents, and various assorted relatives and friends who had come along to share in this most special occasion.

But no Tony.

Emma tried to suppress her disappointment and hurt. She was determined nothing should spoil her enjoyment and valuing of the confirmation.

Roxie, meanwhile, was regretting too late her choice of shoes. What if she really did fall into the font, or tripped up as she walked towards the Bishop? She chewed her lip anxiously. The prospect, now potentially imminent, didn't seem quite so funny as it had the previous night. Like Emma, she didn't want *anything* to spoil it all.

The music group, which had been doing some pre-service singing, now stopped, and the organ took over for the processional hymn. The congregation stood as the rich, deep notes filled the church, everyone began to sing, and the procession with the Bishop bringing up the rear began to move down the aisle.

A nervous swarm of butterflies swept through Roxie's stomach, and she reached nervously for Emma's hand. Emma gave Roxie's fingers a reassuring squeeze. The butterflies did a final swirl, then disappeared. In their place, came a calm certainty that this was going to be a very special and important moment in, and for, her life; and that, if she really, really believed it was so, and owned it, then it would become a reality.

Rosie liked the new order of words for the Baptism and Confirmation Services. 'They're strong and powerful,' she had said to Emma at the rehearsal.

'Do you reject the devil and all rebellion against God?' the Bishop asked. Together with all the other candidates, and the parents and godparents of those to be baptised, Emma and Roxanne responded, 'I reject them'.

'Do you renounce the deceit and corruption of evil?'

'I renounce them.'

'Do you repent of the sins that separate us from God and neighbour?'

'I repent of them.'

The Bishop continued, 'Do you turn to Christ as Saviour?'

'I turn to Christ', they responded.

'Do you submit to Christ as Lord?'

'I submit to Christ.'

'Do you come to Christ, the way, the truth and the life?'

'I come to Christ.'

The Bishop stood before Roxie and made the sign of the cross on her forehead. She looked up, and saw he was smiling down at her. 'Roxanne, Christ claims you for his own. Receive the sign of his cross', he said. A few minutes later, as she watched him bless the water in the font, Roxanne could still feel the mark of the cross on her forehead, as if it had been branded there. Then, again with the others, she made her three-fold declaration of belief in the Christian faith.

'Do you believe and trust in God the Father?' the Bishop asked them all.

'I believe in God, the Father almighty, creator of heaven and earth.'

'Do you believe and trust in his Son Jesus Christ?'

'I believe in Jesus Christ, his only Son, our Lord, who was conceived by the Holy Spirit . . .'

'Do you believe and trust in the Holy Spirit?'

'I believe in the Holy Spirit . . .'

Emma, Roxie, Darren and the other candidates spoke the words clearly and with conviction.

Emma watched with bated breath as Roxie moved forward for the baptism, tottering uncertainly on her precarious shoes. 'Dear God, *please* don't let her fall in the font!' she prayed urgently.

As Roxanne's turn came, the Bishop asked her, 'Roxanne, is this your faith?'

Roxanne managed to whisper, 'Yes, this is my faith.'

A lump came into Emma's throat as the Bishop poured the water three times over the front of Roxie's head, in time with his words: 'Roxanne Marie, I baptise you in the name of the Father, and of the Son, and of the Holy Spirit.' Then he placed a lighted candle in her hand, saying, 'God has delivered us from the dominion of darkness and has given us a place with the saints in light.'

'Shine as a light in the world to the glory of God the Father', everyone in the church responded.

The confirmation candidates lined up in pairs, ready to go forward for the moment of their confirmation. Emma and Roxie walked forward together, and knelt on the cushions in front of the Bishop.

'Emma, God has called you by name and made you his own. Confirm, O Lord, your servant with your Holy Spirit.' Emma felt the pressure of his hands upon her head, and the power of the words. She was profoundly aware that this was a very special and mystical moment. But there was no sense of heat, like Roxie had spoken and prayed about the previous evening. In fact her head felt quite cool and clear.

'Roxanne, God has called you by name and made you his own. Confirm, O Lord, your servant with your Holy Spirit.'

Then the girls stood up and began to make their way back to their places. Roxanne touched Emma's arm, and pointed discreetly. Squashed between a very large woman and the end of a pew, and craning his neck to see from behind an imposing pillar, was Tony! When he caught Emma's eye, he grinned cheerily and did a thumbs-up. Her heart did a little skip of pleasure as she smiled back. 'Ace!' she whispered to Roxie, as they sat down. 'He came!'

'Tony! In a church! And in a suit! I hope you feel suitably – ha, ha, joke! Suit, suitably, get it? – honoured. That is, if you haven't died of shock first', Roxie whispered back. 'Emma! Did you feel it? I did! It was like – like liquid fire running right through me! It was a-mazing!'

Emma gazed at her glowing, excited face, and managed to smile brightly. 'Oh . . . great', she whispered, then bent her head as if in prayer. But no words would come. All she could think about was that it hadn't happened to her. Was there something wrong with her? Was it because she hadn't believed strongly enough that it would happen? Or had she taken it for granted that, if it happened to anyone, it would happen also for her? She truly was glad for Roxie. She really was. 'But – but, if it happened for her, why not for me too?' she questioned silently. 'After all, I was the one who specially encouraged her.' It didn't seem fair really, somehow. Emma struggled with a feeling of jealousy. 'Don't be stupid!' she scolded herself. 'Just because you've been a Christian longer doesn't mean you're going to be more special in God's eyes. God loves everyone the same. Please, Jesus, take away this bad feeling. Please breathe your Spirit of peace and healing into my mind and heart', she prayed over and over, like a mantra.

Words from the story Jesus told of the Lost Son rang as clearly in her head as if she was hearing him at that very moment, recounting it especially to her, especially for her . . . She remembered that it was a story about a son who had returned home, sadder and wiser, after wasting all his inheritance money. His father had been so happy to see him that he had laid on a big celebration. However, the older son wasn't too thrilled at all about this, saying that his father hadn't bothered throwing parties for him ever, even though he had always been a model son and had always served his father faithfully.

Now Emma seemed to hear the words of the father's reply, as if spoken directly to her: 'Emma, my daughter, you're with me all the time, and all I have is yours. But this is a really special, wonderful time and so we must celebrate with Roxanne. Your sister has come home. Roxie has found the Path of Life.'

The ache in Emma's heart melted away and peace slipped softly in to fill its place. She looked up, to find Roxie gazing anxiously at her.

'It didn't happen for you, did it? Me and my big mouth. I'm so sorry', she whispered sadly, as they stood up to sing the next hymn. Emma smiled at her. 'It's OK. Really it is. It's all been perfect', she whispered back. 'Just exactly the way it was meant to be for each of us.'

Roxanne watched as the Bishop said the Prayer of Consecration over the bread and wine: '. . . who, in the same night that he was betrayed, took bread and gave thanks: he broke it and gave it to his disciples, saying, "Take, eat; this is my body which is given for you; do this in remembrance of me". In the same way, after supper he took the cup and gave thanks; he gave it to them, saying, "Drink this, all of you, this is my blood of the new covenant, which is shed for you and for many for the forgiveness of sins. Do this in remembrance of me."'

The church in which the service was taking place used incense. As the wraiths of blue haze swirled and curled softly around the altar, it added to the mystical sense of the celebration of communion. Roxanne remembered being told once that incense represented and symbolised everyone's prayers rising up to God.

She thought it was a nice idea, and wished it was used sometimes in her church. 'It's just so important', she mused silently, 'for us to share in each other's way of doing services. We all worship one God. He has made us all different, but he loves us all equally – so there can't be only one right way to worship him. When you go to someone else's church, often the words of the service take on a new and fresh meaning again, because they're said in a different setting.'

Roxie watched as the girl carrying the incense swung it expertly, so that it gave off just the right amount of smoke. 'I bet God is more worried about the way some Christians are so suspicious of any other Christians who are different from themselves', Roxie's thoughts ran on, 'than he is about a load of other stuff some Christians think is so important. What is the point of being a Christian in the first place, if we can't love and respect people for who they are – even if that is different from ourselves . . .'

Roxanne's thoughts were interrupted by her row getting up to go forward for communion. She and Emma knelt side by side at the communion rail and received the bread and wine for the first time. Emma gazed up at the beautiful stained-glass window behind the altar, with its image of the risen Christ at the centre. The sun slanted through the coloured panes, sending dancing prisms of rainbow-coloured light upon the newly confirmed.

'Now you are in me, and I am in you', she whispered softly. 'Take my life, all that I am and hope to be, and use it to your greater glory.'

The ruby-coloured wine caught at the back of Roxie's throat, and made her cough. She went bright red with the effort to hold back the sound. In comparison with all that she'd experienced at the moment of her confirmation, this bit seemed a bit of an anti-climax. No thoughts or prayers shaped themselves into words behind her closed eyes but she felt, nevertheless, that she was praying. The very fact she was there, being confirmed and receiving her first communion, was a prayer in itself. Roxanne remembered her conversations with the others in the confirmation group on this subject of silence; of the importance of listening out for God, and giving him the space to talk as well. She had a vivid mental picture of God desperately searching for a chink, a pause, in her endless chatter in order to say a few words, and she grinned to herself.

The Bishop caught her now-opened eyes and smiled back. He, in his turn, sent up a quick arrow prayer of gratitude that Roxanne seemed to be having such a happy and positive experience. 'And I pray that her sense of fun and joy will stay always with her, and be a golden thread throughout her life, Amen. There are too many of us Christians who give the overwhelming impression that our faith is an awful burden, instead of an incredible and wonderful gift', he mused, as he prepared to give the consecrated bread to the next line of people kneeling down.

The service had ended, and the newly-confirmed stood outside chatting and laughing with their families and friends.

'You look lovely, my dears', said Emma's grandmother, giving them both a hug. 'When I was confirmed, we all had to wear white dresses, socks, shoes, and a white veil. It was all very…very…'

'White?' asked Emma.

Her gran laughed delightedly. 'Exactly – very, very white.'

'We are so proud of you, Roxie', said her father, handing her a wrapped box. 'A little gift from your mother and me, to mark this very special occasion.'

Roxie pulled away the paper, opened the box and, inside, on a bed of cotton wool, lay a lamb. As she held it up, the light was caught by its cut glass edges and then reflected back out in myriad shades of dancing colours. 'The Lamb of God that takes away the sins of the world', Roxie said softly, turning it this way and that, and setting new rays of colour spinning off its surface each time she did so. 'Thanks, Mum, Dad. What a brilliant present. It's beautiful. It really is.'

Emma was equally pleased with the present her parents had given her. It was a book she'd wanted for a long time, a book of poetry, prayers, meditations and artwork, by a whole variety of Christian writers, poets and artists through the ages. Both girls already possessed Bibles, so they were extra pleased to be given something different.

'Huh! I'll never see you again once you get your nose stuck into this', sighed Roxie, watching over Emma's shoulders as she turned the pages in delight.

Emma, Roxie and Darren stood talking about the service to the other newly confirmed teenagers at the reception organised by the host church.

'Hey, Tom and Clare,' Darren said. 'Did it feel weird – kind of back to front – being one of those who's had communion before confirmation?' Tom paused for a moment, chewing his lip, thoughtfully.

'Nope,' he replied, eventually. 'It was good separating the two. It felt . . . it felt like you didn't have to go through some ritual or ceremony before you could, you know, sit with Jesus at his table. It felt like Jesus accepted me totally as I am, even before any bishop laid their hands on my head.'

Clare agreed. 'Also, having already received communion for some time now, I felt like I could understand and appreciate and value my confirmation more because, well, because I knew already from experience what it was all about.'

'Well, I thought it was perfect for me, just the way it was,' sighed Roxie contentedly.

'I didn't feel *any*thing', mourned another of the group, nibbling at a very crumbly sausage roll and sending a shower of pastry flakes everywhere. 'Not a thing. It was one big anticlimax, so far as I was concerned. I was so disappointed. Perhaps it was my fault'.

'No, I'm sure it wasn't', comforted someone else. 'It didn't live up to my expectations either, and I so wanted it to, as well. And I really made such a huge effort during the service to make it all feel meaningful'.

'Just because you didn't feel exactly the way you expected, doesn't mean that God saw it that way. I bet it was meaningful to him', said a third. 'Just the fact that you were confirmed must be saying heaps, so far as he's concerned.'

'I suppose', said the first one who had spoken, doubtfully. 'Thanks for trying to make me feel better, anyway.'

As the conversation progressed, it became clear what a wide range of feelings, emotions and so on – from nothing to everything – had been experienced by the group.

Liz, one of the clergy, and the person who had prepared Emma, Roxie, Darren and some of the others for confirmation, joined them. When she heard what they were discussing, she said, 'Special experiences like you're talking about are a gift from God. And they usually seem to be given to those whom God feels would specially benefit from them at any particular time.'

Emma remembered the words she had felt were being spoken to her during the service, as she was struggling with her feelings of jealousy.

'Such experiences are not a sign of status, or that one person is better, more holy or whatever than another', Liz continued. 'So, the thing is to live in hopeful trust and expectation that God will bless you as and when he sees fit – and not to worry when something special happens to others, but not to you, at any particular time. It's not a sign of being a second-class Christian, and being of less worth or value in the eyes of God. What is really important is that you concentrate your energies on becoming the person God wants, and has always intended, you to be.'

PART TWO

The day after their confirmation, the girls were in Emma's room sorting through their confirmation notes and deciding what to do with them.

'You know, Roxie, these aren't half bad,' commented Emma, lying on her stomach on her bed, chin cupped in her hand, and flipping the pages over as she spoke. 'You forget how much there is until you look through them again. They're really ace; ever so interesting.' She read out various bits as they caught her eye.

Roxanne, meanwhile, was arranging her notes into various piles, then rearranging them into a different order. After doing this a number of times, she stood back at last, head on one side, and surveyed the final result with a pleased air.

'There! Got it sorted!' she declared proudly. 'I've put it all into three sections. Look. The first section has all the baptism, confirmation, communion, and worship notes and so on. The second is all about praying, etc. And the third is about looking forward, and living your faith, and being a follower of Jesus. You've got to admit it, Emma. I'm really rather brilliant – Oh, yuk! That's gross!', she screeched, as Emma's well-aimed sock wrapped itself around Roxie's face.

Baptism is . . . _____

. . . a service of initiation.

Some people also call it a christening: literally a 'Christ-ing' of the person. But the Bible always calls it baptism. Whichever word you use, though, the meaning is the same.

Baptism is a ceremony of beginning, or becoming. The person being baptised is 'put through' the waters of baptism to begin a new life of belonging to Christ. They are no longer their own, but Christ's:

> Our firm decision is
> to work from this focused centre:
> one man died for everyone.
> That puts everyone in the same boat.
> He included everyone in his death
> so that everyone could also be included
> in his life, a resurrection life,
> a far better life than people ever lived
> on their own.
> Because of this decision,
> we don't evaluate people by what they have
> or how they look.

> *We look inside, and what we see*
> *is that anyone united with the Messiah*
> *gets a fresh start, is created new.*
> *The old life is gone; a new life burgeons!*
> *Look at it!*

> All this comes from God
> who settled the relationship between us and him,
> and then called us to settle our relationships
> with each other.
> 2 Corinthians 5:13f *The Message*
> (Author's italics)

People can be baptised at any age. Jesus himself was baptised as a grown man, at the beginning of his public ministry, by John the Baptist in the River Jordan. And Jesus made it clear to his disciples that, after his death, he wished them to baptise those who turned to him. So, from the day of Pentecost, this is what the disciples did. On the day of Pentecost, when the disciples had received the Holy Spirit, Peter turned to the crowds who had gathered, and said:

> 'Change your life.
> Turn to God and be baptised,
> each of you,
> in the name of Jesus Christ,
> so your sins are forgiven.
> Receive the gift of the Holy Spirit.'
> Acts 2:38 *The Message*

In baptism, God promises to forgive our sins. Baptism is what the Church calls a 'sacrament'. A sacrament is a pledge. It is a promise from God.

A sacrament has been described as an outward and visible sign of an inward and spiritual grace. In baptism, the outward sign is the washing in water. The inward, spiritual grace is the forgiveness of sins, the gift of the Holy Spirit, and birth into new life.

All Christian Churches recognise baptism in water as central to becoming a member of the Church. In the Anglican, Methodist, Roman Catholic and many other Churches, children are usually

BAPTISM IS . . .

baptised as babies. But in the Baptist, House Church movement and other Churches, people can only be baptised as adults, after they have made a full declaration of faith.

Baptism is an inner as well as an outer act. It is about turning your heart to God, and dedicating your life to him. And the service of baptism is both the means, and the expression, of this turning. It is a way of showing by your actions what is in your heart, as well as being an initiation ceremony. On its own, baptism doesn't make someone a Christian. It has also to be worked out in day-to-day living, and growing in the Spirit. You need both.

Jesus, in fact, taught his disciples that what a person was really like inwardly was much more important than mere outer religious observance.

To be a Christian who is growing in the Spirit and in your faith, you also need to go to church on a regular basis if you possibly can.

Although it may seem like it, baptism is not a naming ceremony. Names are fixed in other ways. Baptism is not a kind of magic, either. Nor is it an insurance policy to ensure you go to heaven when you die. God loves everyone, and his love is not 'switched on' by baptism – or 'switched off' if there is no baptism. God's Spirit rests where it will, but God does not force himself upon us, either. He waits, like a courteous and sensitive guest, for us to invite him into our lives, our hearts, our souls.

When a baby is baptised, the parents and godparents make the statements of belief on behalf of the child. Then hopefully, one day when the baby is old enough, she or he will want to make their own declaration of faith by being confirmed . . .

Confirmation is . . . _____

. . . the retelling of the meaning of baptism for those who have already been baptised.

So, all that has just been said about baptism and what it is, also applies to confirmation.

Babies grow up and, sometime during their teens, young people have to sort out their own views on what they believe. Now they have to make up their own minds.

Those who decide to be confirmed publicly take on the promises which were made for them, and on their behalf, at their baptism. Now they have to confirm, and to own, these promises for themselves.

When the bishop places his hands on the head of the person being confirmed, it is a sign of God's power coming into that person's life. The bishop prays that God will confirm – or strengthen – the candidate by the power of his Holy Spirit. This power of God will help them to be true to the promises made, and to live a Jesus-filled life.

Just as with baptism age is no barrier and people are confirmed when the time seems right, usually from pre-teens onwards. It is not something you have to have done whilst you are young, or else you have missed the chance: the right time is when it feels right for the person concerned.

The Bible uses various word pictures to describe what happens when someone becomes a follower, a disciple, of Jesus. It's like:

- being washed clean when you are dirty
- going from a dark room into the sunlight
- becoming friends with someone really special
- being born all over again.

During the confirmation service, you are asked to say that you repent of your sins, and that you turn from evil. Why do we need to turn from evil in order to lead a Christian life? Well, we are part of a fallen world; a world which has gone wrong, and which has drifted well off the course God planned for us. It is a world full of self-centredness and frustration; a world which is altogether in a bit of a mess. However much we do to make the environment, and society, better and more equal – although extremely important – it is still not enough. The problem, Jesus said, lies within each one of us. It's from inside ourselves that the evil thoughts and plans come:

> Jesus said,
> ' . . . nothing that goes into someone from outside
> can make that person unclean,
> because it goes not into the heart
> but into the stomach
> and passes into the sewer . . .
> It is what comes out of someone
> that makes that person unclean . . . '
> Mark 7:18-20 NJB

In baptism and confirmation, you are forgiven by God because of the death of Jesus on the cross. You have been 'washed' and 'made clean' from sin. You have turned away from sin, and turned to living for God. Because of the resurrection of Jesus, you can share a new 'risen' life. And the Holy Spirit is there to help you do this.

Some people seem to think of confirmation as a kind of full stop, or ending, like getting your life-saving certificate in swimming. It's as if they are saying, 'OK, I've been there; done that; got the T-shirt. Now I don't have to think, or do, anything about my Christian faith any more.' But your confirmation is really only the beginning, the beginning of a lifetime of exploration and learning and growing in the Christian faith. Nobody, not even the wisest, most holy person, can claim to have no more learning to do, no more growing to do.

You may already be taking Holy Communion . . .

Communion is . . . _____

. . . for most Christians, the most important part of worship, when we share the bread and the wine together.

We often mark notable occasions with festive meals. There is something special about all being gathered around a table:

- the talking and the laughter
- the delicious food
- the sharing
- the sense of being part of something extra-ordinary.

On the night before he died, Jesus held a very special meal for his disciples. It was the Feast of Passover, an ancient Jewish festival recalling the Israelites' freedom from slavery in Egypt.

Now Jesus was saying that he was the one who would set us free from another sort of slavery, the slavery of sin. He was going to set us free from everything that binds us, and holds us captive to ourselves and our desires.

In Jesus' day, wine was as common as tea is for us today. So when he took bread and wine, he took two very ordinary, every-day things, and made them very special:

> 'This bread', he said,
> 'represents my body,
> broken on the cross for you'.
> Then he gave thanks for the bread, blessed it, broke it and gave it to his disciples. After this, he gave thanks for the wine, and said,
> 'This wine represents my blood,
> poured out for you in my death'.
> Again, he blessed it, and gave it to his disciples.

Whenever the minister celebrating communion repeats these special words of Jesus over the bread and the wine, they come to represent and symbolise for us Christ's body and blood – just as they did for the first followers of Jesus. We celebrate Holy Communion because Jesus commanded us:

'Do this in remembrance of me.'

Jesus was crucified because of human sin: the evil that separates humankind from God and makes it impossible for people to share life with God. Jesus was dying the death, the separation from God, which is the result of sin: he was dying our death. He died for love of us. Jesus said at the Last Supper:

'No one can have greater love
than to lay down his life for his friends.
You are my friends,
if you do what I command you.'
John 15:13,14 NJB

It is called 'communion' because, knowing their sins are forgiven, Christians can come close to Jesus through this sacrament. The structure and words of the communion service, as used in all the major Churches, can be traced right back through the centuries, to the practice of the first Christians.

Although it is the one service, it goes under a number of names, each reflecting a different emphasis of understanding of communion and of worship:

- The word communion means sharing with God and with each other. It is like a family meal, and the emphasis at a 'Service of Holy Communion' is on simplicity, community and fellowship.
- The Lord's Supper is so-called because it is a remembering of the last supper Jesus shared with his disciples. It is seen as a sacrificial meal, reminding us of Jesus' passion and death, and the emphasis is on dignity and solemnity.
- Eucharist comes from a Greek word meaning 'thank you'. The

eucharist is a party, and the emphasis is on much celebration and festivity. In the eucharist thanks is given for the whole of creation and for everything God has done for us in Christ.

- The Breaking of Bread is a service which is usually very simple in style, at which the bread is broken and shared, and the wine is also shared.
- The Mass is a word used in Catholic churches, among others. The word comes from the Latin 'missa', meaning 'Go!' which is used at the conclusion of the service. The people are sent out, at the end of the service, to take what they have received into the world. The word 'Mass' reminds us that Holy Communion is for a purpose. It is to strengthen us for the journey.

Holy Communion – or the Eucharist, the Mass, the Lord's Supper, the Breaking of the Bread, whatever is your preferred title – is a service with many meanings:

- Christians are sharing in the forgiveness the death of Jesus brings, and the new life of the resurrection.
- Jesus is 'food and drink' to Christians. In the service, we are declaring we are one with him, and we hope and want to live our lives in the strength of Christ.
- The Church is not a group of separate individuals, but one family, one body.

So, when we receive the bread and wine of communion together at a service, we are underlining the fact that all of us are part of the one body of Christ, the Church:

> When we drink the cup of blessing,
> aren't we taking into ourselves the blood,
> the very life,
> of Christ?
> And isn't it the same
> with the loaf of bread we break and eat?
> Don't we take into ourselves

the body, the very life,
of Christ?
Because there is one loaf,
our many-ness becomes one-ness –
Christ doesn't become fragmented in us.
Rather, we become unified in him.
We don't reduce Christ to what we are;
he raises us to what he is.

1 Corinthians 10:16f *The Message*

Just as Jesus has accepted and loved us, and we have each become a child of Christ, in the same way we should accept and love his other children. Our God is a God worthy of everlasting praise. He has blessed us so abundantly, pouring his gifts of love out upon the just and the unjust alike. In return, we who know him should offer back up to God all that we are, and hope one day to be, each time we worship.

At the centre of our faith is the cross of Jesus. One piece of the cross is vertical, and points us to friendship and communion and belonging with God. The other piece is horizontal, and points us to communion and friendship and belonging with each other.

Christians look forward to the time when the whole of humankind will recognise that Jesus is Lord, and when good will finally have triumphed over evil.

Jesus died.
But he also rose again from death.
We, too, can share in the risen life,
the new life, of Jesus as his Easter People . . .

Easter people are . . . _____

. . . Christians, who can experience the power of the risen Christ, our living Lord, day by day in our own lives.

After the crucifixion, the disciples were broken people, trapped by their fear, not sure of what to do or where to go. But then God broke through into their lives once more:

> On the evening
> of that first day of the week,
> when the disciples were together
> with the doors locked for fear of the Jews,
> Jesus came and stood among them and said,
> 'Peace be with you!'
> The disciples were overjoyed
> when they saw the Lord.
>
> Again Jesus said,
> 'Peace be with you!
> As the Father has sent me,
> I am sending you.'
> And with that he breathed on them and said,
> 'Receive the Holy Spirit.'
> John 20:19-22 *NIV*

He raised them up from the tombs of their despair. He transformed them into people liberated from their fear, full of the hope and promise of Easter.

Jesus appeared again to his disciples several times over the next forty days, and spoke to them about the Kingdom of God:

> On one occasion,
> he gave them this command:

> 'Do not leave Jerusalem,
> but wait for the gift my Father promised,
> which you have heard me speak about.
> For John baptised with water,
> but in a few days
> you will be baptised
> with the Holy Spirit.'
> Acts 1:4 *NIV*

And so it was, on that great and wondrous day of Pentecost:

> They had all met together,
> when suddenly there came from heaven
> a sound as of a violent wind
> which filled the entire house
> in which they were sitting;
> and there appeared to them tongues as of fire;
> these separated and came to rest
> on the head of each of them.
> They were all filled with the Holy Spirit.
> Acts 2:1-4, *NJB*

'When the Holy Spirit comes upon you,' Jesus had promised, 'You will be filled with power and you will be my witnesses.'

They had become Easter People.

We, too, are Easter People. We are called to look always beyond ourselves, however often we get it wrong despite all our best efforts, to the liberating and redeeming love of God in Jesus Christ.

At each communion service we worship, celebrate and give thanks, in the broken bread and the poured-out wine, for this gift of new life . . .

Worship is . . . _____

. . . literally, reverent homage or service paid to God. Thus, all our private prayer, everything that we offer prayerfully up to God, can be called worship.

As Christians, though, we are called to be members of the body of Christ. So, taking time out with others, in order to give praise and thanksgiving to God for all he has done for us and for all he has given us, is also a very important aspect of worship.

Private and public worship are two sides of the same coin.

'Do you have to go to church to be a Christian?' is a question often asked. Well, you'll certainly be missing out if you don't go. Sometimes people are unable to attend church for various reasons, for example, they are housebound, or very limited in their ability to get around. Of course, they are still Christians. However, for the rest of us, there are all sorts of reasons why it is important that we go to church regularly:

- As followers of Jesus we are called to go on an exciting and complex journey of discovery. For that we need advice from others on the best route.
- We are called to grow in our faith. To do that we need others to walk with us, explore with us, and to help us develop our understanding of what it is to be a Christian.
- It is very hard indeed to be a Christian on your own.
- To be a Christian means to have a special living and growing relationship with God and with other people.

If we go to church and become a regular member of that community, that family, we can:

- make friends with other Christians
- learn more about our Christian faith together
- pray together
- praise and worship God together

- take Holy Communion together
- grow in our faith together
- support, encourage and help each other
- travel together and help keep each other on the right road.

Young people are a vital part of the Church. Older people may have the kind of wisdom which only comes through years of living and learning and experiencing; but young people often have a freshness of vision and a clear-sightedness which has not had time to become clouded by habit and particular ways of seeing and doing things. So:

- do be an enthusiastic member of your church
- join in with what's happening
- ask what you can do in practical ways
- and, if you have a good idea, share it.

Young people are the Church of today, as well as the Church of tomorrow. St Paul described the Church as being like a body. And, like a body, different parts are essential if it is going to live a full life. It would be no good, he said, if it were all eyes, or all feet:

> You can easily enough see
> how this kind of thing works
> by looking no further than your own body . . .
> A body isn't just a single part
> blown up into something huge.
> It's all the different-but-similar parts
> arranged and functioning together.
>
> If Foot said,
> 'I'm not elegant like Hand, embellished with rings;
> I guess I don't belong to this body,'
> would that make it so?
> If Ear said,
> 'I'm not beautiful like Eye, limpid and expressive;

I don't deserve a place on the head,'
would you want to remove it from the body? . . .
No part is important on its own.
Can you imagine Eye telling Hand,
'Get lost; I don't need you'?
Or, Head telling Foot,
'You're fired; your job has been phased out'? . . .

The way God designed our bodies
is a model for understanding
our lives together as a church:
every part dependent on every other part . . .
If one part hurts,
every other part is involved in the hurt,
and in the healing.
If one part flourishes,
every other part enters into the exuberance.
1 Corinthians 12:14f *The Message*

We have all been baptised into one body by the same Spirit of God:

By means of [Christ's] one Spirit,
we all said goodbye
to our partial and piecemeal lives.
We each used to independently call our own shots,
but then we entered into
a large and integrated life
in which *he* has the final say in everything . . .
Each of us is now a part of his resurrection body,
refreshed and sustained at one fountain –
his Spirit –
where we all come to drink.
1 Corinthians 12:12,13 *The Message*

Sometimes, we can come to worship more with a dreary sense

of duty in our hearts than a feeling of happy anticipation. And then it feels like we have very little to offer God at all. But that's not the important thing. What is important is that we are responding to God's call within our hearts.

All through the Bible are stories of people whose thoughts were very far from worship when God made his presence felt in their hearts and lives:

- God spoke to Jacob in a dream.
- Moses did not expect to be confronted by a burning bush. His thoughts were very much elsewhere. But the encounter was to turn his life around.
- The shepherds in the fields were sheep-minding, and probably yarning the night away, when the angels gave them the good news of the birth of the Messiah.
- The disciples were busy catching fish, when Jesus walked into their lives – and things were never the same again.

One of the central threads of our relationship with God should be talking with him regularly or, in other words, praying . . .

PART THREE

Talking with God:
prayers and reflections _____

Confirmation

Jesus –
  now I belong to you!
Take my life,
    all that I am
    and hope to be,
    and use it to
    your greater glory.

May the promises
  I made at my confirmation
  be lived out
  in my life.

          May the joy of that day
            run like a golden river
            through all my days.

  May my life be
    a jam-packed yell of praise;
    a roller-coaster ride
    of celebration,
    that you have called me
    to follow you.
  Amen.

I praise you!
I praise you, God!
I praise you
    with all that I am.
With the whole of my being!
Amen.

Dear God –
  It's like a complete new start!
    A whole new beginning to my life.
    It's like I've been born again!

    The Wind of the Spirit
      has blown right through
        and swept away
          all the bad bits.

    I'm cleansed and renewed.
      It's such a special feeling.
        Help me now to live it out.

      May all that I am,
        and say, and do,
          be a song of praise to you.
          Amen.

    Jesus -
      I used to think
        – before I became one –
        that being a Christian was boring,
        and only for those
        who had nothing better
        to do with their time.

Now I know different!
You truly are
  the best thing
  that's ever happened to me.
You said:
  'I have come
  so that you may have life
  in all its fullness.'*
Well, that's the life I want,
  one which is filled to overflowing
  with you.
Amen.
*John 10:10

Holy Communion

Jesus –
you died for me.
Your body
is the broken bread
I share in Holy Communion.
Your spilt blood
represented in the wine.

But you defeated death.
And no earthly rock
could contain you.

Because of you,
I am raised up, too.
Thank you
for the gift
of eternal life.
Amen.

Jesus –
  when I take communion,
    I feel like I'm reaching back
      to that very first time,
        to that Last Supper.

          'This is me,
            given for you.'

                May my life be
              as bread which is shared
            so that others might live.
          Amen.

            Jesus –
    through the bread
and the wine
  of communion,
    I am in you
      and you are in me.

        It's a holy mystery
          how a small piece of bread
                and a sip of wine
            can fill me with your presence.

          You are the Bread of Heaven;
            bread of our world too.
          May my own life
        nourish and feed
      those who are in need.
    Amen.

All messed up inside
Jesus –
when I'm feeling
all messed up inside,
I come to you
and you heal me.
Thank you!
Amen.

Holy ground
Jesus –
wherever you are
is holy ground.
You are everywhere,
so all places,
all people,
are blessed
by your presence
and your gentle touch.

May I always remember
that wherever I am
you are there before me.
May I treat all places,
all people,
as your holy ground.
Amen.

Lead me where you will
Holy Spirit of God –
live in me.
Take my hand.
Lead me where you will,
just as you led Jesus.
Make me strong for the journey.
Never let me go.
Amen.

You're always with me

Jesus –
    when you left your disciples
      you promised to send your Spirit,
        so that they would never be alone.

When I'm feeling lonely –
    like I am now –
      help me to remember
        that your promise
          holds true for me as well.

Thank you for your Spirit
    which dwells within me,
      guiding and directing
        my every step,
          and comforting me
            when I'm feeling down.
            Amen.

Make me wise

Spirit of Wisdom –
make me wise.
Help me to see truly and clearly.
In all the decisions of my life,
may I know God's wish and will for me.
Amen.

Serving others

Jesus –
    you showed us
    that in serving others
    we build your kingdom
    here on earth.
Teach me to see
    and to serve you
    in all whom I meet.
And may I do it
    with a joyful heart.
Amen.

The needs of others

Jesus –
    I'm always quick to recognise
    and to pray for my needs.
Help me to be as mindful
    of the needs of others,
    both in my prayers
    and in my actions.
Amen.

Your timing, not mine

Heavenly Father –
    it's *hard* to be patient
    when you're *itching* to get on
    with all that's out there to do,
    in a world *filled* to the brim
    with opportunity
    and excitement!

Help me to trust,
and to *really* believe,
that you will show me
what you want me to do,
when the timing is right
for me
and for you.
Amen.

Your will, not mine

Dear God –
you know
what I want.
You also know
what I need!
So –
I'll just leave it
up to you to decide
what's best.
You're more likely
to get it right
than me!
Amen.

Living Flame of Love

Living Flame of Love,
burn within me.
Remove all
that is selfish,
and bad,
and not of you.
Amen.

Bridge-building and peace-making

Why *can't* we all get on?
Why *do* people *always* take sides?

It's almost as if we *need* enemies
to make us feel superior;
to make us feel we really belong
to a particular group.

I don't want to be part of all that.
Help me to be a peacemaker,
like *you* were, Jesus.
Amen.

Jesus –
when quarrels and arguments divide,
help me to be a bridge-builder,
a reconciler and a healer.
Give me the words
to make things better.
Amen.

We've quarrelled

Oh, Jesus!
we were *such* good friends,
and it only started
as a *little* argument.
But now it's grown so huge
it's like we're deadly enemies.

How *could* it have got
to be this big?

Please show me what I should do
  to help make things right,
  and to change things back
  to how they were before.
Amen.

Take away the bad feelings

Healing Lord –
N. . . and N. . .
have quarrelled.
There's so much hate in the air.
Take away the bad feelings
and the hurt of their angry words.
Soothe away their pain.
Please draw them back together again.
Amen.

It's great again!

Hey, Jesus!
It's all OK!
In fact, it's great.
We've made up.
We're friends again.
Thanks!
Amen.

May the fruits of the Spirit grow in me

Jesus –
  love
    joy
      peace
  patience
kindness
  goodness
    faithfulness
      humility
    self-control . . .

It's an awesome list!

But I pray, even so,
  that all of these fruits of the Spirit
      will take root
        and grow in me.

    You are the Living Water,
  who can bring to ripeness
the driest seeds of the desert.
  When I drink of you
  my life is changed.

So nourish me.
  Make me fruitful
    in your service.
      Amen.

When the going gets tough

When the going gets tough,
   it's tempting to give in
   and to give up.
That's when I need you,
   Jesus,
   more than ever.
Give me stickability.
Keep me faithful
   to what I have to do –
   just as you were.
Amen.

Hold me steady and true
Father –
   it's hard sometimes to know,
   amongst all the amazing possibilities,
   the confusing and tempting
   choices and voices,
   how to keep my balance;
   to know what's right for me.
So hold me steady and true.
May I keep my eyes
   fixed always on you.
Amen.

Be my guide
   Jesus –
     walk
  before me.
    Walk

beside me.
When the map of life
confuses,
guide me safely
along the right path.
Amen.

Help my understanding

There's *such* a mystery
about you, Lord.
The more I find out,
the less I seem really to know!
Learning about you
is a never-ending voyage of discovery.

And yet –
you are
far, *far* closer to me
than I am to myself.
You are
my most intimate companion.
You love me
from the inside out.

Help me
to see you everywhere.
Help me
to know you in everyone.
Help my understanding.
Amen.

As you love me
Dear God,
   thank you
      for loving me
         like you do.
            Knowing it
               makes each day
                  glowing and bright.

                     Fill me
                  to overflowing
               with your love,
         that I may
      love others
   as you love me.
Amen.

                     All I think, say, do
                     Father –
                  may all that
               I think,
            I say,
               I do
                  today,
                     be pleasing
                        to you.
                           Amen.

Getting my priorities right

How on earth did you manage,
  Jesus,
  to get your priorities right?
Didn't you ever get confused
  about which thing to do first?
How *did* you fit it all in?

        I mean –
          teaching,
          preaching,
          healing,
          raising
          – and you *still* found time to pray!

            Is that the answer, then?
            Prayer soaked each of your days,
              and each of your tasks
              was surrounded with it.

          It came as naturally to you
            as breathing in God's air.

Teach me that way of praying.
May all that I think, say, do,
  be a kind of prayer to you.
Amen.

Don't get too close

Jesus —
sometimes,
I hold you at a distance,
I know I do.

It's because
I'm frightened,
if you get *too* close,
you'll want more of me
than I'm prepared
to give.

That, in fact,
you'll demand my all,
and then there'll be
nothing
left for me.

So —
help me to trust.
Help me
to understand.
Help me
to know
that in giving my life
over to you,
I find my true freedom.
Amen.

It's not fair!

Jesus!
It's just not fair!
How could you
let it happen?
If you're so powerful,
do something.
Please!
Amen.

It's hard being a Christian

Jesus –
it's really hard and lonely sometimes,
isn't it,
walking the Christ-path.
And especially
when people name-call
and jeer at what you believe.

They don't understand
about you
and all that you've done –
for them
as well as for me.

Give me
the words
with which to answer them.

Make me
a courageous witness
to your love and your truth.

Help me
find other young people
to travel the Christ-path with me.
Amen.

Trust

Jesus –
I can really relate
to that story about Peter who,
when he took his eyes off you,
began to sink into the stormy water.*

So, please help me always to place
all my trust in you, even when
– *especially* when –
life is feeling rough and the going is tough.

I know you love me
and want the very best for me.
I place everything and all that I am
– my life, my hopes, my dreams –
into your caring hands.

Help me to keep my eyes fixed on you.
Help me to walk on water.
Amen.
*Matthew 14:22f

Forgiveness

Jesus –
    as you hung on your cross,
    you prayed that
    those who had so hurt you
    would be forgiven.

I'm hurting, too,
    both inside and out,
    from what was done to me.

Help me to forgive them.
    Help me to let go
    of the anger I feel.

Help me also to know
    how I should respond,
    and what I should do,
    if there is a 'next time'.
Amen.

Dear Jesus –
Thank you
for helping me to forgive.

    Thank you
    for setting me free
    from the darkness
    of that bitterness and hurt.

    Thank you
    for making the sun shine again.
    Amen.

Jesus —
you didn't always
turn the other cheek, did you?

You chose your moment,
and you responded
in the way that was best
for that particular occasion.

Make me wise like you,
and with the same insight.
Help me to know when to react
and what I should do.

If I stand up for myself when necessary
then I'm more likely to do it
for others as well.
Amen.

Dear God —
my heavenly parent.
Forgive me.
I'm so *sorry*
for what I said and did.
Please forgive me.
Help me
not to do it again.
Amen.

Dear God –
Thank you
  for forgiving me!
Thank you
  for the sense
  of peace
  and of wholeness
  your forgiveness brings!
Amen.

Justice
Dear God –
I was standing
  by a rushing river today,
  and I remembered how you said
  in the Bible
  about justice flowing like water,
  and righteousness
  like a never-failing stream.*

There are so many suffering people
  of one sort or another.

That's the most terrible injustice,
  isn't it?

So I pray for them,
  each according to their need.

Show me what I can do
  to help justice to flood our world
  – your world.
  Amen.
  *Amos 5:24

Courageous witnesses
Dear God,
I pray for those
who struggle to live out
and to spread your Word,
despite heaps of setbacks
and difficulties.
May they always know your love
surrounding and supporting them.
Keep them strong.
Keep them safe.
Amen.

Make me a courageous witness, too
Jesus –
I came to know you
through other people.
Thank you for them!
May I have the courage
to make you known to others
  in my turn.
Amen.

God's family

Dear God,
   my heavenly parent,
both mother and father to me,
   one of the most ace things
about being a Christian
   is that now I have *two* families –
the one I was born into;
   and the family of those
who follow you.
   Thank you for them all.
Help me to be
   a loving and caring member
of both.
   Amen.

Dear Jesus –
     you prayed that
         we would all be one,
             just as you and the Father are one.[*]

So, how sad you must be
  at all the divisions
     and splits;
        all the arguing
           over such silly things
              which really aren't important at all,
                when all's said and done.

I pray for your divided Church.
  May we learn to be one,
     the way you originally meant
        and dreamed for us to be.
          Amen.   *John 17:22, 23

I don't understand me – but you do
Jesus –
    I don't understand me,
at all
      – and nor does anyone else,
it often seems.

    But *you* do.

In all this confusing time
    of growing up,
stay close by.
    Guide me.
Keep me safe.
    Amen.

It's no use pretending with you
    Jesus –
    you know me
    through and through.
    It's no use
    pretending with you.

    With you, I can say it
    – or shout or scream it! –
    just the way it really is.
    Just the way I really feel.
    That's so ace.
    Thank you!
    Amen.

A light in the dark

God –
  life is really hard
  just at present.
Be a light for me
  in the dark.
A strong hand to hold.
Amen.

Words – and silence

Creator God,
  I read somewhere
  that words should grow
  out of your silence
  if they are to be life-giving
  rather than destroying.

I think of the words you spoke
  into the silent chaos
  of a world waiting to be born.[*]
  And I think I understand.

May I always remember
  words are a precious gift from you.
May I never use them as weapons.

Teach me the value of silence
  if I have nothing creative to say.
Amen.
*Genesis 1:1f

Jesus –
you knew when to speak
and when to be silent.
Teach me that all-important lesson.
Amen.

Holy Spirit of God –
teach me to listen,
as well as to talk,
when I pray.

Perhaps *you* might have
something important
you want to say to *me*!

In the space
and in the silence,
I will be able to hear it better.
Amen.

Any time, any place
Jesus –
you are
my constant
and faithful
and loving
friend.

Any time.
Any place.
Wherever
I am.

Whatever
my need.
I know
you hear me.
I know
you are near me.
I thank you
and I praise you!
Amen.

At the beginning of the day

Jesus –
   I offer today,
   with whatever it may bring,
   as a gift to you.

Take it and bless it.

Walk through it
   with me.
May all I say, all I do,
   be worthy of you.
Amen.

At the end of the day

Dear God!
Wow!
What a day it's been!
Full of so many people
and experiences
and so much to thank you for.

Forgive me the things
I didn't handle so well.
Help me to do better next time.

Thank you for sharing it all.
Thank you for guiding me
and keeping me safe.
Amen.

Oh, Jesus!
My day didn't go too well,
did it?
Not the way I planned,
at all.
And I don't suppose
it thrilled you too much,
either.

But I guess that,
if I hand the bad bits
over to you,
you can straighten them out
and redeem them
and make more of it all
than I did.

Help me
not to be too down
about today.
Help me
to do better tomorrow.
Amen.

For a particular moment

Jesus –
stay close by.
I *need* you.
Amen.

Jesus –
may the right things happen.
May *your* will be done.
Amen.

Dear God,
guide me.
Fill me
with your wisdom.

Fill me
with your strength.

Surround me
with your love.
Amen.

Life is just so amazing!

Oh, God!
Most holy and wondrous God!
I think I'll burst
with all these feelings
bubbling up inside of me!

Your world is so full of wonder
and beauty

75

and colour
and mystery
and promise
of all that is yet to come.

Life is just so amazing!
And it's so brilliant
to be alive
here,
now,
at this moment in time.

Thank you!
Thank you for my life
and for all your other gifts
in creation.

Thank you
for your love
which has turned my world
inside out
and upside down.
Amen.

The future

Dear God,
    once I used to think
    it'd be nice to know the future.

But now I see
    that it's not such a great idea,
    after all!

If I could predict it,
    then I'd be tempted
    to find my own ways
    of getting through,
    rather than trusting it to you
    to plan the best route.

So –
    Creator
    and Lord
    of life,
    and of this fantastic world,
    I place my future
    – with all its possibilities
    and all its promise –
    into your hands.

You know the way.
Keep me sensitive
    to your wish
    and your will for me.

Make the road straight.
Keep my footsteps true.
May my whole life
    be a close dance with you.
Amen.

Ways to pray _____

The first thing to say is that there is no one set way to pray, nor one set sort of prayer. There is just one, *really important*, rule. And that is that we must always try to be absolutely honest in our prayers – to speak it just the way it really is: whether it is a heartfelt song of happiness; a yell of joy and thanksgiving; a cry of anger, sadness, or bewilderment; or a request for ourselves or someone else. Trust God to accept it all, the whole lot. He wants to hear, and to share, the good bits *and* the bad bits. Prayer should be an enjoyable and precious time, not a boring obligation.

Each one of us is unique and unrepeatable: fingerprints and DNA are proof of that. Equally, our prayer relationship with God will be special and unique.

We may think that we pray when we feel like it. That it is our initiative. But, actually, prayer begins with God:

> Jesus said,
> 'You did not choose me,
> no,
> I chose you . . . '
> John 15:16 *NJB*

God is constantly praying in us, speaking to us, and softly knocking on the door of our hearts. When we feel the urge to pray, we are answering this invitation. It's a bit like responding to a softly, but insistently ringing telephone. As with a phone conversation, it is very important that we don't do all the talking, and so prevent God from getting a word in edgeways. About 50:50 is a good split. Once we get into the habit of listening to God, we can often find what he has to say to us is very surprising indeed.

Prayer is both the easiest, and the hardest, thing in the world. It's hard because it demands honesty and commitment. It's easy because it's like coming home to an always-loving parent. As with such a parent, we can tell it just the way it is, just the way it really feels, knowing that whatever we do say will be understood and valued. Like anything worthwhile, it does need working at, if we are going to go deeper and deeper in our relationship with God. But the pay-off makes it all worth it.

There are as many ways of praying as there are human beings. One way to begin to pray is just to open your mind and heart, and to say exactly and honestly how you feel, using ordinary, everyday language. You don't need special or fancy words. Just lay everything out before God. Ask him for his understanding and wisdom, his strength and healing, to come into those things and situations which you have shared. Then ask that his wisdom and understanding, his strength and healing, will be his gift to you.

On certain occasions, your prayer time will be taken up with some very particular or specific thing which you want to share with God. That's fine. But try also to remember to pray regularly for other people and situations, and just to spend time praising God and thanking him for all that he has done for you, and given you.

It's hard to concentrate your mind and to pray when your body is feeling restless. When this is so for you, you might like to try the following:

- Sit in a comfortable, supportive chair, with your legs uncrossed, and your hands resting in your lap.
- Close your eyes, and concentrate first on making your breathing steady and even.
- Now work your way down your body in your mind, beginning at the top of your head, and concentrating on each area. Any area where you notice tension, imagine as a block of ice, a knotted rope, or a coiled spring. Then imagine it melting, unravelling, loosening.
- Return to your breathing. As you breathe in, think the word 'Jesus'. As you breathe out, think the word 'me'. This, in itself, is a prayer.

- Now you are relaxed, just listen to what God wants to say to you in the silence of your heart. If you want to speak to him, do so.

Another creative way to pray is to take a few words of scripture which you really like; read them over several times, letting the words sink into your mind and your heart. If any particular word, phrase or image particularly attracts your attention, stay with it for as long as feels helpful. If your mind begins to wander, don't worry. Just bring the thoughts into what you're doing, and let them mingle and mix together. In this way, you are letting the word of God enter into your everyday joys, preoccupations, worries, anxieties, longings, dreams and so on. Now you can make a prayer out of the mixture.

If you have a vivid imagination – and even if you haven't! – you might especially like to do the following:

- Take a Gospel passage, and read it several times until it is familiar to you.
- Close your eyes, and imagine the scene is happening now, at this moment, and that you are an active part of it all. Imagine the heat, the smells, and so on.
- Picture who is present, what they are saying, and what they are doing. Join in with them.
- Talk with the characters in the scene.
- Talk with Jesus. Speak to him from the heart, simply and honestly. Tell him what is in your heart, share with him your deepest wishes and longings.
- Listen to what Jesus is saying to you.

One of the nicest things at the end of the day is to think back on all that has happened. This can also be a great way to pray:

- Ask God to be with you.
- Play the day back to yourself, looking first at those moments you've especially enjoyed.

- Relive them and their happiness, and thank God for them. They are God's gifts to you and signs of his love.
- Don't self-judge, just thank God.
- Every day is full of different moods and inner feelings. Run your mind back over those you remember. Again, don't judge them or yourself. Just ask God to help you understand them, and what caused them.
- Thank God for having been in all the events of the day, and for inspiring you to be your best self.
- If you feel that there were times and events in the day where you did not respond to God, and were less than he would have wished, ask for his forgiveness, knowing that he will always give it.
- Finally, ask God's guidance for tomorrow, and entrust yourself to God's goodness, '. . . like a child in its mother's arms' (Psalm 131).

God can be found in all things: a photo, a picture, a lit candle, an object you look at or hold, newspapers and magazines, a flower . . . in fact, anything in God's creation can be an aid to getting yourself into prayer.

Try to establish a regular time of prayer, as it's very easy for it to get pushed out when life gets busy. Find a time of day, and try to stick to it. Although we can pray anywhere, anytime, it can be very helpful to have your own special place, where you go for your regular prayer times.

And don't forget your Bible. Read it regularly. That, too, is a form of praying. You may find bible-reading notes are helpful. Go and have a browse in your local Christian bookshop; ask others in your church, and/or your minister, what they recommend. There is quite a wide variety available. Use ones that you feel comfortable with, but which also challenge you, so that you grow in your understanding and your faith.

The Psalms are a wonderful source of material for prayer, full of all the emotions we all feel, and reflecting the struggle of the writers to come to terms with a whole range of negative feelings, such as anger and desire for revenge.

For Jesus, prayer was a way of life. Being rooted in prayer gave him the knowledge of God's will for him; and the wisdom, the direction, the strength and the courage he needed in order to carry it out. And prayer can be the same for us too, if we want it to be.

PART FOUR

Looking forward: living your faith as a follower of Jesus _____

Followers of Jesus are called 'Christians' because this was the nickname given to the first disciples of Jesus, and the name has stuck ever since. It means 'a follower, a disciple, of Jesus Christ'. A Christian is someone who has put their faith in Jesus, the risen Lord, and who tries to live out his teachings in their own life.

Christians are Easter People. They are Easter People because they can experience day by day, in their own lives, the power of the risen Christ, their living Lord. They are Easter People because they are called to live out this resurrection life of Jesus in their own lives. For Easter People, faith and action go hand in hand. You cannot have one without the other, as the following extract from James reminds us:

> Act on what you hear!
> Those who hear
> and don't act
> are like those who glance in a mirror,
> walk away,
> and two minutes later
> have no idea who they are,
> what they look like . . .
>
> Does merely talking about faith
> indicate that a person really has it?
>
> For instance,
> you come upon an old friend

dressed in rags and half-starved and say,
'Good morning, friend!
Be clothed in Christ!
Be filled with the Holy Spirit!'
and walk off without providing
so much as a coat or a cup of soup –
where does that get you?

Isn't it obvious that God-talk
without God-acts is outrageous nonsense? . . .
Faith and works, works and faith,
fit together hand in glove.
James 1:22f *The Message*

So, what difference does it make, being a Christian? Well, life is full of choices. Some are relatively easy, like which film to go and see. Some can be a bit harder, but not life-threateningly important, like what clothes to wear for a special occasion. Some decisions are difficult and important. The choice made may affect our life for some time. The decision may not be always – or entirely – our own: parents, teachers, or others, may be part of what is finally decided. And sometimes there is no choice. Then, we just have to get on with what is there to be done.

But being a Christian, a follower of Jesus, is something we freely choose to do, or not do, as the case may be. God does not force us. The decision is ours.

When we have made the choice and the decision, baptism and confirmation are important ways of publicly affirming what we have chosen and decided. We are declaring that we have nailed our own colours to the cross of Christ.

Our Christian faith is like a mustard seed which, if watered and attended to, will grow into the biggest of all plants. This is what James is saying in the Bible passage quoted above. The seed of our faith is watered and nurtured by:

- praying
- reading the Bible, and other books which help us on our journey
- going to church, and taking part in the life of our Christian community
- declaring our faith by our actions, by the way we live our lives.

All of God's desire and will for us is summed up in 16 words:

> Love God
> with all your heart,
> and love others
> as much as
> you love yourself.

The bit about loving yourself is extremely important. Some people make the serious mistake of thinking that it is a holy thing to despise yourself, your body and who you are. Nothing could be further from the truth.

We are told we are made in God's image and, even if that image gets very misshapen indeed, it still has the potential for transformation back into God's likeness. We are also told that God loves each one of us with the tender and all-embracing love and care of the best parent. So we should not devalue or despise what God values and cherishes and loves.

God dwells within each one of us. Our bodies are temples of his Spirit. Most of us are dissatisfied with some aspect of our bodies and the way we look, and wish we were different in one way or another. Either we think we're too fat or too thin; too tall or too short; hair the wrong colour, thickness, too curly or too straight; and so on and so on. A certain amount of dissatisfaction is fine, as it acts as a spur for us to make the best of ourselves – whether it is of our bodies, our brains, our gifts or our situation. However, too much dissatisfaction can block our growth into freedom of mind and heart – a freedom that God is constantly calling us to. Also, if all our energy is turned in on ourselves, we will have none left for anyone or anything else.

The teens are a time of great physical, mental and emotional change, and it's hard to keep track of all that's happening. It can feel like you're on a rollercoaster, and the majority of teenagers spend a lot of time being unhappy or dissatisfied about one aspect or another of themselves. However, like most things, it's a question of balance. A sense of humour is important, as it helps to keep things in proportion. To be able to laugh at ourselves and not take ourselves too seriously is a very good thing.

Following Jesus gives us daily challenges and daily blessings. God is constantly beckoning us from beyond ourselves. He is constantly calling to us, and gently encouraging us on:

- to reach for the stars within ourselves
- to be more gentle and compassionate
- to be more loving and caring
- to be less selfish
- to be more forgiving
- to be more truthful.

In fact, to grow in our likeness of him.

It can be hard to go against the crowd, and the Christ-path can sometimes feel lonely for one reason or another. We usually know what is right, and what is wrong. The trouble is doing it. Rules by themselves are not enough, as St Paul well knew:

> ' . . . I need something more!
> For if I know the law but still can't keep it,
> and if the power of sin within me
> keeps sabotaging my best intentions,
> I obviously need help!
>
> I realise that I don't have what it takes.
> I can will it, but I can't *do* it.
> I decide to do good,

but I don't *really* do it;
I decide not to do bad,
but then I do it anyway.

My decisions, such as they are,
don't result in actions.
Something has gone wrong
deep within me
and gets the better of me every time . . .

Is there no one
who can do anything for me?

. . . The answer, thank God,
is that Jesus Christ can and does.
Romans 7:9f *The Message*

When we ask for God's help, we are far more likely to choose what is right, and then to have the strength to carry it through.

To be a Christian does not mean to have a religious part to our lives. Rather, it is the *whole* of our lives – whatever we do – which is affected by our relationship with God.

Jesus' cross really is an amazing symbol. It teaches us so many things:

• It reminds us of the love, and the courage, and the unswerving dedication to his God-calling which led Jesus to the cross.
• It reminds us of a love that took him beyond death into the everlasting arms of the Father. That, through his death, he has defeated death.
• It reminds us that we are called to live his risen life, empowered by his Spirit, in this God-created, God-given world.

When we look at the cross, we see both a vertical and a horizontal beam. The vertical beam directs our attention to our relationship with God through Jesus. The horizontal beam directs our attention to our relationships with each other and the world through Jesus.

If we allow our lives to flow through Jesus to God, and through Jesus to other people, we will be purified, strengthened and empowered by him. And, as our lives flow into him, his life will also flow through us into a world desperately in need of his light and of his love:

> God can do anything, you know,
> far more than you could ever imagine
> or guess
> or request
> in your wildest dreams!
>
> He does it
> not by pushing us around
> but by [God's Spirit]
> working within us.
> Ephesians 3:15f *The Message*

When, despite all your best efforts, you still get it wrong, as we *all* do, don't be too discouraged. Just pick yourself up, dust yourself down, offer it all up to God, and start over again. It's not so much the falling, but the asking for forgiveness, the resolve and the resolution to do better the next time, which is really important.

Simon Peter, one of Jesus' most devoted and trusted followers for the three years of his public ministry, discovered this. On the night before Jesus' death Peter, along with the other disciples, ran away and left Jesus alone when he was arrested. Then, a few hours later, Peter denied three times that he knew Jesus. When Peter realised what he had done, he was beside himself with grief and remorse. But then, with the knowledge of Jesus' forgiveness, and in the power of the Spirit, he became Peter the Rock upon which the early Christian Church was built.

Don't be discouraged if you go through periods of doubt or

cynicism, or any other difficulty with believing in, or living out, your faith. It's not a sin to feel like this, and it happens to us all. It is a sign of growth, rather than of fading away, because faith is different from knowledge. To question, to face and admit your doubts honestly, takes courage. These are important staging posts in your Christian journey.

Don't struggle on on your own. Share your questions, difficulties, worries, fears, or whatever, with God. Ask for his help, strength, wisdom, and guidance. God knows all about how you feel long before you do, anyway. But it is still important to pray about it. Share it with other Christians so that they, too, can help and support you.

Any exciting and worthwhile journey of discovery has low as well as high points, and the Christian journey is no different. And, like any earthly exploration, unless you carry on in faith, you'll not see that amazing view just around the next corner. So, don't give up! Here's a prayer to help you . . .

> When the going gets tough,
> it's tempting to give in
> and to give up.
> That's when I need you,
> Jesus,
> more than ever.
> Stay very close by.
> Give me stickability.
> Keep me faithful.
> Hold me steady and true.
> May I always keep
> my eyes fixed on you.
> Amen.

Jesus wants us, above all else, to be real and to be genuine. To be real and genuine makes us aware; aware of ourselves and of others. When we are truly aware, we can appreciate every aspect of God's glorious creation, and can sense his touch upon all that he has brought into being. When we are real, we are connected with our needs. Real – genuine – aware – real: the circle of need is completed; and the beginning is connected with the end.

And our biggest need, without a doubt, is Jesus.

I get down on my knees
and ask God's Spirit
to strengthen you
and that Christ
will live in you
as you open the door
and invite him in.

adapted from Ephesians 3:14 *The Message*

The Last Word _____

'Hey, Roxie! What an ace day!'
  'Yeah, Emma. It was totally cool!'